AF440920

20 HAMBURGER RECIPES FOR ALL TASTES

Burger Recipes, How to Combine Burger Ingredients, Burger Ingredients Benefits, Burger Curiosities.

Copyright © Heinrich Fischer Fuch

Dear Reader:

Thank you for purchasing this precious book! We are glad that you have found what you are looking for.

This greeting is to thank you for being part of our loyal family of readers. We are so grateful for your purchase, because we wouldn't be here without loyal readers like you.

He could have chosen any other Book, but he chose ours. So we really appreciate that you made that decision.

Thanks again and enjoy!

Our goal is that you are always satisfied. We hope to see you again in our next editions, which I personally assure you will be more pleasant.

We would be very happy if you would take a minute of your time to rate our book on the "Amazon.com" page (it is the same page where you bought this book), and at the same time express your opinion in the comments, so that other people that look for the same thing that you were looking for, can find it more easily.

Have a great day!

Sincerely,

Heinrich Fischer Fuch and team.

Heinrich Fischer Fuch

INDEX

20 BURGER RECIPES FOR EVERYONE

The combination of its flavors makes it simply irresistible, and it's hard to imagine it could be more delicious. However, with these**20 hamburger recipes**We show you that this dish can improve by a lot.

Best of all, these hamburger recipes that we share work for all tastes, so you will find a wide variety of flavors and textures. You are going to crave them all!

ORIGIN OF THE BURGERS

The history of this dish goes back to the German city of Hamburg, where a steak made from ground beef, known as "Hamburg-style steak", quickly became popular.

During the s. XIX a large number of Germans emigrated to the United States, where it is believed that this steak began to be eaten between two loaves, and that it became a fashion in the town of Hamburg, located in New York.

The hamburger quickly became one of the most popular foods, due to its ease of preparation and because the industrialization of the time favored its production.

The brothers Richard and Maurice McDonald are responsible for the hamburger becoming the queen of fast food, after opening their first restaurant in 1940, specializing in the preparation of this dish.

CURIOSITIES ABOUT THE BURGER

o   For US Americans, the hamburger is a type of sandwich, the only difference is in the**Ground beef**circular.

o   The most popular meat for making a hamburger is**beef**. It is estimated that 80% of hamburgers are prepared with this meat.

o   The Heart Attack Grill restaurant, located in Las Vegas, offers the "World's Baddest Burger" and not because of its taste, but because of its caloric content of approximately 9,982 calories. Would you dare to eat it?

- The hamburger lost popularity when famous presenter Oprah Winfrey declared that she would never try a hamburger again. And their influence is such that beef prices fell at such a statement. Even so, it is still an irresistible dish!

HOW TO COMBINE THE BURGER INGREDIENTS

- Instead of ground beef, use chicken.

- Add finely grated potato, zucchini or carrot; Aside from enhancing the flavor, the meat will yield a bit more, and it's a good trick for kids to eat the veggies!

- Change the lettuce leaves: one day use the romaine, another the orejona, then French, etc., because believe it or not, the flavor varies subtly from one to another.

- To really make it look like a different dish, substitute the bun with pita or box bread in its different options (multigrain, white, whole wheat).

o   In addition to the classics**ketchup**and mayonnaise, add soy sauce, mustard or mayonnaise flavored with chipotle, thousand island dressing or other.

BURGER RECIPES

BURGER WITH FRIED FISH

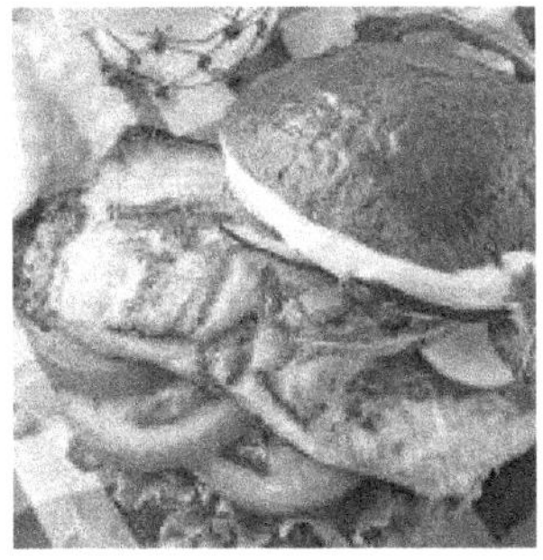

Looking for easy fish fillet recipes? Here we show you how to prepare this Lenten burger, the favorite of the season!

CRAB BURGER WITH GARLIC SHRIMP

Indulge yourself this season by preparing a crab burger with garlic shrimp, very delicious!

MINI BURGERS FOR SNACKING

You'll love how easy it is to learn this mini burger recipe that you can enjoy anytime.

AVOCADO BURGER

This avocado burger option is perfect for those who are looking for a meatless, breadless, yet delicious option.

ARABIC BURGER

Today we want to share with you a very original, delicious and oriental-flavored touch: prepare this Arabic burger with our super easy and delicious recipe. You will not regret! You are interested: Vegan menu: salad ...

FRIED CHICKEN BURGER

Nothing better to satisfy the craving of the week than a delicious fried chicken burger. If you are also savoring it, keep reading and take note of the recipe. ...

GREEK BURGER WITH GRUYÈRE CHEESE

We know that you love trying different flavors of your favorite dishes, and you are going to love this one: we invite you to try a Greek burger with Gruyère cheese, exquisite! You're interested in: Salad ...

VEGETARIAN BURGER RECIPE WITH PORTOBELLO

Who said you couldn't enjoy the taste of a burger if you're veggie? Here we bring you a recipe vegetarian burger with portobello that you are going to suck on ...

CLASSIC CHARCOAL BURGERS

This time is perfect to organize a barbecue. Do you already know which dish you can't miss? These delicious classic charcoal burgers! Follow the recipe step by step ...

RECIPE BURGERS WITH PORK MEAT

We know they are your favorite dish, and that is why we teach you how to make them super delicious: try these recipe burgers with pork. You are going to fall in love with his ...

MINI LAMB BURGERS WITH GOAT

CHEESE

Your barbecue party is approaching and you cannot miss delicious sandwiches to accompany the moment. Surprise everyone with these mini lamb burgers with goat cheese, ...

MINI BURGERS FOR PARTIES

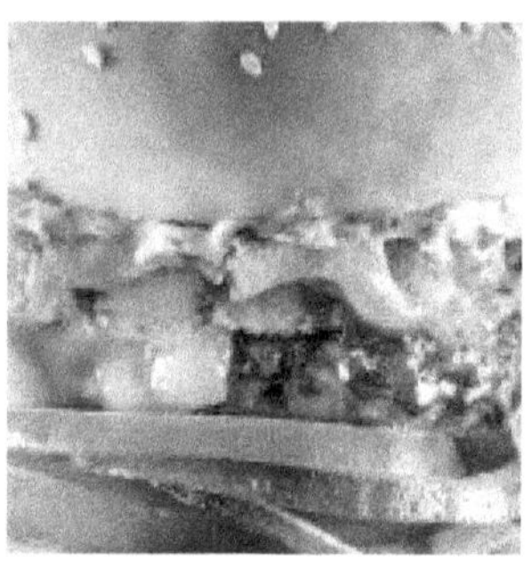

Snacks are a must at a celebration! That's why we bring you these mini burgers for parties, so delicious that they will conquer the palate of your guests. Everything…

MINI BURGERS FOR KIDS

There are many delicious ways to pamper the little ones in the house, but nothing like these mini burgers for kids. Know the recipe and surprise them.

MAKE A VERY DELICIOUS AND

HEALTHY VEGETARIAN BURGER

There are no excuses for you to enjoy your favorite food. We present you a delicious vegetarian burger, with the exact ingredients that make it very healthy. Do not stay with ...

MEXICAN BURGER WITH

GUACAMOLE

Forget the diet completely and decide to prepare a delicious Mexican burger with guacamole. You will suck your fingers! Know the ingredients you need and let's cook! Are you interested in reading: ...

CHICKEN AND MUSHROOM BURGER

We all love hamburgers and the various and original ways they are created, but we bet you have never eaten a delicacy like this ...

GARLIC AND ROSEMARY BURGER

WITH CARAMELIZED ONION

Are you starving? The solution is with this garlic and rosemary burger with caramelized onion. Irresistible and super delicious. We don't want to be a bad influence but with this recipe ...

BBQ MINI BURGERS

Enjoy these mini BBQ burgers with your friends or family at any time, you do not need special occasions to prepare them, since they go very well with everything and, the best thing, they are ...

CHICKEN BURGUER

Nothing better to satisfy the craving of the week than a delicious chicken burger. If you are also savoring it, keep reading and take note of the recipe. ...

CRUNCHY CHICKEN AND

GUACAMOLE BURGER

How long have you not eaten a mega crunchy chicken and guacamole burger? At home you can also enjoy something this big and super filling. Are you hungry yet? ...

BURGER WITH FRIED FISH

INGREDIENTS

- 4rye burger buns
- 4Italian lettuce leaves
- 1tomato in slices
- ½ cup mayonnaise
- tworadishes in thin slices
- 1cup of wrinkle leaves
- 4pieces of sea bass fillet 170 g each
- twotbsp. Of olive oil
- twotbsp. of butter
- 1minced garlic clove

o   4pickled gherkins with slices

INSTRUCTIONS

1.   Salt and pepper the fish fillets, grill in a pan over medium heat with the olive oil, when you turn the fish add the garlic and butter.

2.   Assemble the burgers with the lettuce, tomato, fish mayonnaise, radish, arugula and pickles.

- TIME: 30m

- SERVINGS: 4 servings

BENEFITS OF ROBALO FISH

o   It contains potassium, a mineral necessary for the health of the nervous system and muscular activity.

o   It is rich in magnesium, which helps the intestine function properly and improves immunity.

o   It is high in vitamin B complex.

o   It has a mild laxative effect.

o   Snook is one of the most versatile fish in the kitchen, you can make a wide variety of dishes with it.

CRAB BURGER WITH GARLIC SHRIMP

CONSENT YOUR ANTOJO THIS SEASON BY PREPARING A CRAB BURGER WITH GARLIC SHRIMP, VERY DELICIOUS!

INGREDIENTS

- 4hamburger buns
- 1cup shredded red cabbage
- 1cup grated carrot
- 3tbsp. mayonnaise
- ½ serrano pepper, chopped

- 500g of crumbled crab or crab pulp
- ½ onion finely chopped
- ½ cup of chopped parsley
- 3eggs
- ½ cup of flour
- 6tbsp. Of olive oil
- 200g miniature shrimp
- 4tbsp. of butter
- twominced garlic cloves
- 1cup of filleted lettuce

INSTRUCTIONS

1. In a hot pan with the butter, quickly sauté the shrimp with the garlic and half the parsley, season with salt and pepper and set aside.

2. Mix the crab meat with the onion, the rest of the parsley, half the egg and half the flour, salt and pepper and form four pancakes.

3. Brown the pancakes in a skillet over medium heat with the olive oil.

4.   Meanwhile, mix the cabbage with the carrot, serrano pepper and mayonnaise.

5.   Assemble the burgers with the coleslaw, crab cakes and shrimp, finish with some lettuce and serve.

- TIME: 40m

- SERVINGS: 4 servings

CURIOSITIES ABOUT CRABS

o   There are more than 4 thousand varieties of this crustacean.

o   They live in almost all regions of the world with beaches. Some remain on the seabed, others in fresh water, or also underground.

o   They eat only fruits and vegetables, which makes them really healthy. Seafarers also eat algae and / or organic matter.

o   Boxer crabs are one of the few species of crabs that are inedible.

o   The famous surimi is made mostly of crab meat, which makes it a rich source of protein, and that you can consume in sushi, salads and other stews.

MINI BURGERS FOR SNACKING

YOU WILL LOVE HOW EASY IT IS TO LEARN THIS MINI BURGER RECIPE THAT YOU CAN ENJOY ANYTIME.

INGREDIENTS

- 8burger buns guys
- 500g of ground beef
- 1leafless lettuce
- 1tomato in thin slices
- 1/2cup pickles, sliced

- 1cup shredded cheddar cheese
- 1cup of grated Manchego cheese
- 1cup of breadcrumbs
- twoeggs
- 4olive oil spoons

INSTRUCTIONS

1.   Mix the meat with the ground bread and egg, salt and pepper. Form balls with the preparation, fill with the cheeses and shape them into a pan size the size of bread.

2.   Grill in a skillet over high heat with the olive oil.

3.   Form the hamburgers with the lettuce, tomato and pickle.

- TIME: 35m

- SERVINGS: 4

CURIOSITIES ABOUT THE BURGER

o   For US Americans, the hamburger is a type of sandwich, the only difference being the circular ground beef.

o   The most popular meat to make a hamburger is beef. It is estimated that 80% of hamburgers, including mini hamburgers, are prepared with this meat.

o   The Heart Attack Grill restaurant, located in Las Vegas, offers the "World's Baddest Burger" and not because of its taste, but because of its caloric content of approximately 9,982 calories. Would you dare to eat it?

o   The hamburger lost popularity when famous presenter Oprah Winfrey declared that she would never try a hamburger again. And their influence is such that beef prices fell at such a statement. Even so, it is still an irresistible dish!

AVOCADO BURGER

THIS AVOCADO BURGER OPTION IS
PERFECT FOR THOSE WHO ARE
LOOKING FOR A NO MEAT AND NO
BREAD, BUT DELICIOUS.

INGREDIENTS

- 4halved avocados
- 1sliced red pepper
- 1sliced green pepper
- 1sliced yellow pepper
- 1sliced orange bell pepper
- 1/2shredded purple cabbage

- 1/2leafless lettuce
- 4thick slices of panela cheese
- 1cup of mayonnaise
- 1I beaten egg
- 1cup of breadcrumbs
- Enough oil for frying
- 1/2cup black sesame

INSTRUCTIONS

1.   Bread the cheeses with egg and breadcrumbs. Fry them in a pan over medium heat with oil and remove the excess fat, reserve.

2.   Remove the skins from the avocados, spread mayonnaise on four halves and place the fried cheese, lettuce, cabbage and peppers.

3.   Finish with the avocado halves without mayonnaise and sesame.

- TIME: 20m

- SERVINGS: 4

CURIOSITIES ABOUT THE BURGER

o   For US Americans, the hamburger is a type of sandwich, the only difference being the circular ground beef.

o   The most popular meat to make a hamburger is beef. It is estimated that 80% of hamburgers are prepared with this meat.

o   The Heart Attack Grill restaurant, located in Las Vegas, offers the "World's Baddest Burger" and not because of its taste, but because of its caloric content of approximately 9,982 calories. Would you dare to eat it?

o   The hamburger lost popularity when famous presenter Oprah Winfrey declared that she would never try a hamburger again. And their influence is such that beef prices fell at such a statement. Even so, it is still an irresistible dish!

ARABIC BURGER

INGREDIENTS

- twocups finely sliced cabbage
- twotbsp. Of olive oil
- 1sliced tomato
- 1/3 cup of chopped parsley
- twotbsp. lemon juice
- 400g of ground beef
- 1/2 tbsp garlic powder
- 1/4 of cup of onion chopped
- 1tbsp. oregano
- 1tbsp. vegetable oil
- 1egg
- twotbsp. ground bread

- 5tbsp. by jocoque
- 1tbsp. from zatar
- 4pieces of arabic bread

INSTRUCTIONS

1. Mix the meat with the garlic, egg, breadcrumbs, onion and oregano. Salt pepper.

2. Form small meat patties and grill them in a frying pan with the oil over medium heat.

3. Mix the rest of the ingredients (except the bread) and season with salt and pepper to taste.

4. Heat the pieces of bread and open them carefully. Garnish with jocoque, stuffed with the salad and meat. Finish with a little zatar and serve.

- SERVINGS: 4 servings

HOW TO VARY THE INGREDIENTS OF THE BURGERS

- Instead of ground beef, use chicken.

- Add finely grated potato, zucchini or carrot; Aside from enhancing the flavor, the meat will yield a bit more, and it's a good trick for kids to eat the veggies!

- Change the lettuce leaves: one day use the romaine, another the orejona, then French, etc., because believe it or not, the flavor varies subtly from one to another.

- To really make it look like a different dish, substitute the bun with pita or box bread in its different options (multigrain, white, whole wheat).

- In addition to the classic ketchup and mayonnaise, add soy sauce, mustard or mayonnaise flavored with chipotle, thousand island dressing or something else.

FRIED CHICKEN BURGER

INGREDIENTS

- 4hamburger buns
- ½ cup mayonnaise
- 4chicken breast pieces cut in half
- ½ cup of flour
- ½ cup of milk
- 1egg
- 1cup of breadcrumbs
- ½ red onion filleted
- 1cup shredded cabbage
- 1grated carrot

o   Enough oil for frying

INSTRUCTIONS

1.   Season the chicken. Mix the flour with the egg and milk, add a teaspoon of salt, pass the chicken pieces through the mixture and then through the ground bread; go back through the mixture and once more in the breadcrumbs.

2.   Fry in hot oil until the chicken pieces are browned.

3.   Meanwhile, combine the cabbage with the carrot and red onion, salt and pepper. Toast the bread, spread a little mayonnaise and finish with the chicken and coleslaw.

- TIME: 30m

- SERVINGS: 4 servings

CURIOSITIES ABOUT THE BURGER

- For US Americans, the hamburger is a type of sandwich, the only difference being the circular ground beef.

- The most popular meat to make a hamburger is beef. It is estimated that 80% of hamburgers are prepared with this meat.

- The Heart Attack Grill restaurant, located in Las Vegas, offers the "World's Baddest Burger" and not because of its taste, but because of its caloric content of approximately 9,982 calories. Would you dare to eat it?

- The hamburger lost popularity when famous presenter Oprah Winfrey declared that she would never try a hamburger again. And their influence is such that beef prices fell at such a statement. Even so, it is still an irresistible dish!

GREEK BURGER WITH GRUYÈRE CHEESE

INGREDIENTS

- 4hamburger buns
- 600g ground lamb
- 1cucumber
- 1egg
- 4tbsp. by jocoque
- twotbsp. natural yogurt
- 100g of feta cheese in small cubes
- 3tbsp. red pepper, roasted and chopped
- 4tbsp. chopped black olives

- twotbsp. minced fresh mint
- twotbsp. Of olive oil
- twotbsp. red onion and chopped
- twotbsp. chopped parsley

INSTRUCTIONS

1.   Mix the ground beef with the egg, chopped onion, and parsley. Season.

2.   Form four meat patties and reserve.

3.   Combine the jocoque with the yogurt, mint and black olives. Salt pepper.

4.   Grill the meat in a very hot skillet with the olive oil. Flip the portion only once so it doesn't dry out.

5.   Help yourself with a peeler and remove long cucumber ribbons.

6.   Place the meat on the bread, spread the jocoque mixture generously over the meat and add the cucumber ribbons, some pieces of pepper and feta cheese.

7.   Finish with a few drops of olive oil and bring to the table.

- SERVINGS: 4 servings

HOW TO VARY THE INGREDIENTS OF THE BURGERS

o   Instead of ground beef, use chicken.

o   Add finely grated potato, zucchini or carrot; Aside from enhancing the flavor, the meat will yield a bit more, and it's a good trick for kids to eat the veggies!

o   Change the lettuce leaves: one day use the romaine, another the orejona, then French, etc., because believe it or not, the flavor varies subtly from one to another.

o   To really make it look like a different dish, substitute the bun with pita or box bread in its different options (multigrain, white, whole wheat).

o   In addition to the classic ketchup and mayonnaise, add soy sauce, mustard or mayonnaise flavored with chipotle, thousand island dressing or something else.

VEGETARIAN BURGER RECIPE WITH PORTOBELLO

INGREDIENTS

- 4hamburger buns
- 4Portobello mushroom pieces
- 1red bell pepper in strips
- 1green bell pepper in strips
- 1yellow bell pepper in strips
- 3tbsp. Of olive oil
- 4Lettuce leaves

- 1cup spinach, cooked and drained
- 1cup of whipping cream
- 1cup grated Parmesan cheese

INSTRUCTIONS

1.   Grill the portobello and the peppers on a griddle over high heat with the oil.

2.   Meanwhile, heat the spinach with the cream and Parmesan; salt pepper.

3.   Toast the bread and assemble with the different preparations.

- TIME: 30m

- SERVINGS: 4 servings

CURIOSITIES ABOUT THE BURGER

For US Americans, the hamburger is a type of sandwich, the only difference being the circular ground beef.

The most popular meat to make a hamburger is beef. It is estimated that 80% of hamburgers are prepared with this meat.

The Heart Attack Grill restaurant, located in Las Vegas, offers the "World's Baddest Burger" and not because of its taste, but because of its caloric content of approximately 9,982 calories. Would you dare to eat it?

The hamburger lost popularity when famous presenter Oprah Winfrey declared that she would never try a hamburger again. And their influence is such that beef prices fell at such a statement. Even so, it is still an irresistible dish!

CLASSIC CHARCOAL BURGERS

INGREDIENTS

- 4 hamburger buns
- ½ cup mayonnaise
- 4 chicken breast pieces cut in half
- ½ cup of flour
- ½ cup of milk
- 1 egg
- 1 cup of breadcrumbs
- ½ red onion filleted
- 1 cup shredded cabbage
- 1 grated carrot
- Oil

INSTRUCTIONS

1.   Season the chicken. Mix the flour with the egg and milk, add a teaspoon of salt, pass the chicken pieces through the mixture and then through the ground bread; go back through the mixture and once more in the breadcrumbs.

2.   Place on the grill until the chicken pieces are browned.

3.   Meanwhile, combine the cabbage with the carrot and red onion, salt and pepper. Toast the bread, spread a little mayonnaise and finish with the chicken and coleslaw.

- TIME: 30m

- SERVINGS: 4 servings

CURIOSITIES ABOUT THE BURGER

o   For US Americans, the hamburger is a type of sandwich, the only difference being the circular ground beef.

o   The most popular meat to make a hamburger is beef. It is estimated that 80% of hamburgers are prepared with this meat.

o   The Heart Attack Grill restaurant, located in Las Vegas, offers the "World's Baddest Burger" and not because of its taste, but because of its caloric content of approximately 9,982 calories. Would you dare to eat it?

o   The hamburger lost popularity when famous presenter Oprah Winfrey declared that she would never try a hamburger again. And their influence is such that beef prices fell at such a statement. Even so, it is still an irresistible dish!

RECIPE BURGERS WITH PORK MEAT

INGREDIENTS

- 1avocado
- ½ cup mayonnaise
- 1serrano chili
- 500g ground pork
- 4tbsp. chopped onion
- 1egg
- 1tbsp. of paprika
- 3tbsp. of oil
- 8mini hamburger buns
- ½ leafless lettuce

- o   1sliced tomato
- o   1sliced cucumber
- o   4tbsp. mustard
- o   4cups banana chips

INSTRUCTIONS

1.   Blend the avocado with the mayonnaise and the chili; salt pepper.

2.   Mix the pork with the onion, egg and paprika, salt and pepper and form eight pancakes with the mixture. Grill the meats in a skillet over medium / high heat with the oil. Reservation.

3.   Heat the loaves in the oven slightly. Form the hamburgers with the meat, lettuce, tomato, cucumber, prepared mayonnaise and mustard.

4.   Accompany with the banana chips.

- ▪   SERVINGS: 4 servings

ORIGIN OF THE BURGERS

The history of this dish goes back to the German city of Hamburg, where a steak made from ground beef, known as "Hamburg-style steak", quickly became popular.

During the s. XIX a large number of Germans emigrated to the United States, where it is believed that this steak began to be eaten between two loaves, and that it became a fashion in the town of Hamburg, located in New York.

The hamburger quickly became one of the most popular foods, due to its ease of preparation and because the industrialization of the time favored its production.

The brothers Richard and Maurice McDonald are responsible for the hamburger becoming the queen of fast food, after opening their first restaurant in 1940, specializing in the preparation of this dish.

MINI LAMB BURGERS WITH GOAT CHEESE

INGREDIENTS

- 150g of goat cheese
- twotbsp. chopped olives
- 1/2 cup onion, chopped
- 300g ground lamb meat
- 1tbsp. minced mint
- 1cucumber, thinly sliced
- 8miniature hamburger buns
- 1egg
- 3tbsp. ground bread
- twotbsp. Of olive oil

INSTRUCTIONS

1.   Mix the lamb with the onion, olives, mint, egg and breadcrumbs. Salt and pepper and form pancakes the size of loaves.

2.   Fry the meat in a skillet over medium heat with the oil, about 2 minutes per side.

3.   Arrange the cucumber slices on the base bread, then the meat, a slice of goat cheese, olive oil and pepper. Close them and take them to the table.

- SERVINGS: 4 servings

ORIGIN OF THE BURGERS

The history of this dish goes back to the German city of Hamburg, where a steak made from ground beef, known as "Hamburg-style steak", quickly became popular.

During the s. XIX a large number of Germans emigrated to the United States, where it is believed that this steak began to be eaten between two loaves, and that it became a fashion in the town of Hamburg, located in New York.

The hamburger quickly became one of the most popular foods, due to its ease of preparation and because the industrialization of the time favored its production.

The brothers Richard and Maurice McDonald are responsible for the hamburger becoming the queen of fast food, after opening their first restaurant in 1940, specializing in the preparation of this dish.

MINI BURGERS FOR PARTIES

INGREDIENTS

- 1honey pineapple cut into slices
- Salt and pepper
- Lettuce leaves, as necessary
- twotomatoes
- 1purple Onion
- 1chives stalk
- twotbsp. Worcestershire sauce
- ½ cup mayonnaise
- 250g of bacon
- 500g of ground beef

- 200g emmenthal cheese
- 8small buns
- ½ tbsp. ground cumin
- 3tbsp. mustard grains
- 1sprig of ground coriander
- 1tbsp. dried oregano
- twotbsp. of paprika
- 1egg

INSTRUCTIONS

1. Process the meat with the egg, the paprika, the mustard, the coriander, the oregano and the cumin, salt and pepper. Shape the patties.

2. Grill the meats, pineapple slices and bacon.

3. After three or four minutes, flip the meat and top with the cheese to melt.

4. Meanwhile, mix the mayonnaise with the Worcestershire sauce and finely chopped chives.

5.   Assemble the hamburgers: put a meat on each base, distribute lettuce, tomato, onion on top, cover with the mayonnaise and close them. It serves.

- TIME: 40m

- SERVINGS: 8 servings

CURIOSITIES ABOUT THE BURGER

- For US Americans, the hamburger is a type of sandwich, the only difference being the circular ground beef.

- The most popular meat to make a hamburger is beef. It is estimated that 80% of hamburgers are prepared with this meat.

- The Heart Attack Grill restaurant, located in Las Vegas, offers the "World's Baddest Burger" and not because of its taste, but because of its caloric content of approximately 9,982 calories. Would you dare to eat it?

- The hamburger lost popularity when famous presenter Oprah Winfrey declared that she would never try a hamburger again. And their influence is such that beef prices fell at such a statement. Even so, it is still an irresistible dish!

MINI BURGERS FOR KIDS

INGREDIENTS

- 300g ground turkey breast
- 3tbsp. chopped onion
- twotbsp. chopped parsley
- 1egg
- twotbsp. Of olive oil
- fiftyg cheddar cheese slices, quartered
- twotbsp. Dijon mustard
- 12mini burger buns
- 1sliced tomato
- 1cup baby spinach leaves

INSTRUCTIONS

1.   Mix the turkey meat with the onion, parsley and egg, salt and pepper and form 10 to 12 pancakes. Grill them in a skillet over high heat with the olive oil. When they are almost done, cover them with the cheese so that it is gratin.

2.   Spread a little mustard on the top of each bread, place the meat on top and finish with the tomato and spinach. Pierce with a toothpick and take them to the table.

- SERVINGS: 10-12 servings

HOW TO VARY THE INGREDIENTS OF THE BURGERS

o   Instead of ground beef, use chicken.

o   Add finely grated potato, zucchini or carrot; Aside from enhancing the flavor, the meat will yield a bit more, and it's a good trick for kids to eat the veggies!

o   Change the lettuce leaves: one day use the romaine, another the orejona, then French, etc., because believe it or not, the flavor varies subtly from one to another.

o   To really make it look like a different dish, substitute the bun with pita or box bread in its different options (multigrain, white, whole wheat).

o   In addition to the classic ketchup and mayonnaise, add soy sauce, mustard or mayonnaise flavored with chipotle, thousand island dressing or something else.

MAKE A VERY DELICIOUS AND HEALTHY VEGETARIAN BURGER

INGREDIENTS

- twocups of beans
- 1cup oatmeal
- twotbsp. parsley
- 1large white onion
- 1pinch of dried oregano

- 1tbsp. olive oil tureen
- Hamburger bun
- 1pinch of salt
- 1pinch of pepper
- 1pinch of garlic paste
- ½ red onion
- ¼ lettuce
- Vegetables and toppings

INSTRUCTIONS

1. Put the beans cooked with the oat flakes in a food processor and process the ingredients well until they are integrated.

2. Add the chopped white onion and parsley. Reprocess until integrated. Add salt, black pepper, garlic paste, and the olive oil. Process until you get a thick paste. Form balls the size of a hamburger meat and transfer to a skillet over medium heat with vegetable oil. Cook for about 5-10 minutes on each side. Toast the bread a little, place the hamburger meat and add red onion, lettuce and the vegetables that you like the most.

- TIME: 40m

- SERVINGS: 4 servings

HOW TO VARY THE INGREDIENTS OF THE BURGERS

- Instead of ground beef, use chicken.

- Add finely grated potato, zucchini or carrot; Aside from enhancing the flavor, the meat will yield a bit more, and it's a good trick for kids to eat the veggies!

- Change the lettuce leaves: one day use the romaine, another the orejona, then French, etc., because believe it or not, the flavor varies subtly from one to another.

- To really make it look like a different dish, substitute the bun with pita or box bread in its different options (multigrain, white, whole wheat).

- In addition to the classic ketchup and mayonnaise, add soy sauce, mustard or mayonnaise flavored with chipotle, thousand island dressing or something else.

MEXICAN BURGER WITH GUACAMOLE

INGREDIENTS

- 600g of ground beef
- 4tablespoons of ground bread
- twoeggs
- 4tablespoons minced onion
- 4Italian lettuce leaves
- 1sliced tomato
- 1/2 red onion sliced
- 4cheddar cheese slices
- 1cup of golden chorizo
- 1yellow corn shelled

- 8browned bacon sheets
- twojalapeno peppers, sliced
- 1/2 cup of guacamole
- 4hamburger bun pieces

INSTRUCTIONS

1.	Mix the ground beef with the ground bread, egg and chopped onion; season and divide into four equal parts. Shape the burgers and grill them on a griddle or grill over high heat with a little oil. When they brown, place a slice of cheese on top to gratin.

2.	Lightly toast the bread and form the hamburger with the rest of the ingredients.

WHAT IS GUACAMOLE

Guacamole is a delicious sauce made from avocado and chili. Its name is derived from the Nahuatl word Ahuacamolli, which I know is made up of the words Ahuacatl, avocado and molli, mole or sauce. Without a doubt, Mexicans love spicy and avocado alike, especially if these two are accompanied and provide us with the great delicacy called guacamole.

Whether alone or accompanied, this MEXICAN SAUCE it can always be in each of our family meals. If you, like us, love guacamole, yes or yes you should know how to prepare it at any cost and there is no better place to learn how to do it than in this book. Proof of this are these great guacamole recipes that we have for you.

Share the guacamole recipe with your mother, aunt or best friend, you can surely make someone very happy with a new dish. Don't forget to leave us your comments and rate the recipes that appeal to you the most.

CHICKEN AND MUSHROOM BURGER

INGREDIENTS

- 4hamburger buns
- 600g of ground chicken
- 1/2cup onion, minced
- 1egg
- 3tablespoons of ground bread
- 1/2teaspoon garlic powder
- 1cup sliced mushrooms
- 1/2cup bell peppers in thin strips
- 4olive oil spoons
- 1/2sliced onion

- 8spinach leaves
- 1tablespoon mustard

INSTRUCTIONS

1. Combine chicken with minced onion, bread crumbs, garlic powder, and egg. Salt and pepper and form square pancakes with the mixture.

2. Cook the meat in a skillet with 2 tablespoons of olive oil.

3. Fry the onion with the pepper and the remaining oil. When they soften, add the mushrooms. Salt and pepper and reserve.

4. Heat the loaves in the oven. Spread mustard on the base bread, place 2 spinach leaves for each hamburger, place the meat and finish with the mushroom stew.

GARLIC AND ROSEMARY BURGER WITH CARAMELIZED ONION

INGREDIENTS

- 500g of ground beef
- 4hamburger buns
- 1tablespoon extra virgin olive oil
- 1large onion, thinly sliced
- 1tablespoon brown sugar
- 1tablespoon balsamic vinegar
- 3tablespoons red wine
- twogarlic cloves finely chopped

- 1finely chopped fresh rosemary branch
- 100g Gruyere cheese, thinly sliced
- 1tablespoon grainy Dijon mustard
- Sanitized lettuce leaves, as necessary
- Salt and pepper

INSTRUCTIONS

1. Cook the onions in the hot oil for four minutes until they begin to soften. Add the muscovado sugar and balsamic vinegar, leave them for another 10 minutes until they begin to caramelize. Add the wine and cook over low heat until it has evaporated, salt and pepper and reserve.

2. Besides, combine the ground beef, garlic and rosemary, and season

3. generously with salt and pepper. Shape the patties with your hands. Heat a lightly greased pan and place on the grill over high heat. Put the hamburgers for three minutes on each side. Add the cheese and let it gratin.

4.   Serve on each bun with a tablespoon of mustard, lettuce, a serving of meat, and the caramelized onions.

BBQ MINI BURGERS

INGREDIENTS

- 500g of ground beef
- 1egg
- 1/4finely chopped onion
- 1tablespoon chopped parsley
- 1/2cup parmesan cheese
- 5tablespoons bbq sauce
- 12mini cream cheese filled buns
- 400g of bacon
- Salt and pepper
- 5tablespoons mayonnaise
- 5tablespoons mustard

INSTRUCTIONS

1.   Mix the meat with the egg, onion, parsley and cheese until integrated, salt and pepper. Shape the meat into balls to the size of the loaf. Flatten them slightly.

2.   Grill the meat to the desired length. Reservation. In another pan, brown the bacon until crisp. Reserve on absorbent paper.

3.   Cut the buns in half and top the meat with a strip of bacon. Spread mayonnaise, mustard, and BBQ sauce on sides or serve with burger.

CHICKEN BURGUER

INGREDIENTS

- 4hamburger buns
- ½ cup mayonnaise
- 4chicken breast pieces cut in half
- ½ cup of flour
- ½ cup of milk
- 1egg
- 1cup of breadcrumbs
- ½ red onion filleted
- 1cup shredded cabbage
- 1grated carrot
- Enough oil for frying

INSTRUCTIONS

4.   Season the chicken. Mix the flour with the egg and milk, add a teaspoon of salt, pass the chicken pieces through the mixture and then through the ground bread; go back through the mixture and once more in the breadcrumbs.

5.   Fry in hot oil until the chicken pieces are browned.

6.   Meanwhile, combine the cabbage with the carrot and red onion, salt and pepper. Toast the bread, spread a little mayonnaise and finish with the chicken and coleslaw.

- TIME: 30m

- SERVINGS: 4 servings

CURIOSITIES ABOUT THE BURGER

o   For US Americans, the hamburger is a type of sandwich, the only difference being the circular ground beef.

o   The most popular meat to make a hamburger is beef. It is estimated that 80% of hamburgers are prepared with this meat.

o   The Heart Attack Grill restaurant, located in Las Vegas, offers the "World's Baddest Burger" and not because of its taste, but because of its caloric content of approximately 9,982 calories. Would you dare to eat it?

o   The hamburger lost popularity when famous presenter Oprah Winfrey declared that she would never try a hamburger again. And their influence is such that beef prices fell at such a statement. Even so, it is still an irresistible dish!

CRUNCHY CHICKEN AND GUACAMOLE BURGER

INGREDIENTS

- 4Chicken medallions
- 1/2 cup of ground bread
- 1/2 cup unsweetened cereal flakes
- 1/2 cup of flour
- 1egg
- 4whole wheat bread rolls
- 1medium container of canned sour cabbage
- 1/2 piece of purple cabbage clean
- twentyg of butter

- twoavocados
- twofinely chopped onion slices
- 1lemon (the juice)
- Oil for frying, the necessary
- Salt and pepper

INSTRUCTIONS

1.   Lightly grind the cereal flakes, combine them with the breadcrumbs. Pass the medallions through a little flour, then through the beaten egg, and then through the bread and flake mixture. Repeat the operation if you want it to be very crispy. Freeze them for 20 minutes.

2.   Meanwhile, cut the red cabbage into strips and sauté it for a few minutes with the butter or until it softens. Salt pepper.

3.   Mash the avocado, mix it with the chopped onion, add the lemon juice and salt and pepper.

4.   Heat enough oil very well. Fry the medallions there until you notice that they brown. Reserve them on absorbent paper.

5.   Serve the meat on buns with the lettuce, sour cabbage, purple cabbage, and guacamole.

WHAT IS GUACAMOLE

Guacamole is a delicious sauce made from avocado and chili. Its name is derived from the Nahuatl word Ahuacamolli, which I know is made up of the words Ahuacatl, avocado and molli, mole or sauce. Without a doubt, Mexicans love spicy and avocado alike, especially if these two are accompanied and provide us with the great delicacy called guacamole.

Whether alone or accompanied, this MEXICAN SAUCE it can always be in each of our family meals. If you, like us, love guacamole, yes or yes you should know how to prepare it at any cost and there is no better place to learn how to do it than in this book. Proof of this are these great guacamole recipes that we have for you.

Share the guacamole recipe with your mother, aunt or best friend, you can surely make someone very happy with a new dish. Don't forget to leave us your comments and rate the recipes that appeal to you the most.

BENEFITS OF EATING CHICKEN

There are many BENEFITS OF EATING CHICKEN Among the main ones are that it is easily digestible, low in fat, rich in vitamins, minerals and contains the essential amino acids that the body needs.

CHICKEN PROPERTIES

For every 100 g of chicken you eat you get:

- 195 kilocalories
- 30g protein
- 7.7 g fat
- 2.2 g of saturated fat
- 0 g of carbohydrates

Dear Reader:

Thank you for purchasing this precious book! We are glad that you have found what you are looking for.

This greeting is to thank you for being part of our loyal family of readers. We are so grateful for your purchase, because we wouldn't be here without loyal readers like you.

He could have chosen any other Book, but he chose ours. So we really appreciate that you made that decision.

Thanks again and enjoy!

Our goal is that you are always satisfied. We hope to see you again in our next editions, which I personally assure you will be more pleasant.

We would be very happy if you would take a minute of your time to rate our book on the "Amazon.com" page (it is the same page where you bought this book), and at the same time express your opinion in the comments, so that other people that look for the same thing that you were looking for, can find it more easily.

Have a great day!

Sincerely,

Heinrich Fischer Fuch and team.

Heinrich Fischer Fuch

www.ingramcontent.com/pod-product-compliance
Lightning Source LLC
Chambersburg PA
CBHW071932120726
48001CB00005B/1952